GREAT ILLUSTRATED CLASSICS

THE HUNCHBACK OF NOTRE DAME

Victor Hugo

Adapted by
Malvina G. Vogel

Illustrations by Pablo Marcos Studios

**BARONET
BOOKS**

BARONET BOOKS, New York, New York

GREAT ILLUSTRATED CLASSICS

edited by
Joshua E. Hanft

Contents

CHAPTER   PAGE

1. Quasimodo, the Pope of Fools 7
2. The Gypsy Girl 19
3. Two Rescues 33
4. A Wedding Night Conversation 49
5. The Bellringer of Notre Dame 57
6. A Trial and Punishment 71
7. Esmeralda's Admirers 83
8. The "Murder" of Captain Phoebus .. 97
9. A Confession and a Sentence 111
10. Sanctuary! 131
11. Gratitude or Pity? 151
12. Waiting for Phoebus 161
13. Swearing Revenge!. 173
14. The Battle for Notre Dame 181
15. My Mother! My Daughter! 203
16. "Everything I Loved!" 229
17. Together in Death 237

About the Author

The sickly infant born to Joseph and Sophie Hugo in Besancon, France, on February 26, 1802 wasn't given much chance to survive. But the boy *did* survive and grew up to become one of the greatest writers France and the world has ever known: a poet, a playwright, a novelist, and a genius at all three. He was Victor Hugo.

During Victor's early years, his mother's love of books and poetry inspired that same love in her son, and his genius was first revealed in his poetry. By the age of fourteen, he had written twenty-three poems, and at fifteen, he received a prize from the famed *Académie Francaise* for a 334-line poem.

Later, when Victor turned to writing historical plays and novels, he used them to speak out on political and social issues he felt strongly about. In *The Hunchback of Notre Dame* and later in his most famous work, *Les Misérables*, Hugo expressed his outrage at France's courts and her prison system.

Because he insisted that his historical works be

researched accurately, he spent three years reading histories of France, exploring the remains of old houses around Notre Dame, and examining every nook and cranny of the cathedral itself.

When it was time to sit down and write *The Hunchback*, Hugo had to meet a deadline or forfeit 1,000 francs for each week the book was late. Hugo loved money and spent it very well, so he wrapped himself from head to toe in a large, knitted shawl, locked away his clothes so he wouldn't be tempted to leave the house, and began his novel. Six months later, in 1831, France welcomed *The Hunchback of Notre Dame*, and Victor Hugo welcomed a lot of money!

Because he championed many political causes, some popular, others not, Hugo was forced to spend twenty years in exile. But he returned a hero and was elected to the *Académie Francaise*—the highest honor France can give a writer!

When Victor Hugo died on May 22, 1885, at the age of 83, an entire nation mourned. His body lay in state under the *Arc de Triomphe*. Then a procession of two million Frenchmen followed the simple black hearse along a route hung with flags inscribed with the names of his famous works. France buried her beloved poet in the *Panthéon*, with honors usually reserved for a king!

A Noisy Crowd

CHAPTER 1

Quasimodo, the Pope of Fools

On the morning of January 6, 1482, the people of Paris were awakened by the deafening peals of all the church bells in the city. Not only was it a religious holiday, but it was also the Festival of Fools, and Parisians celebrated it by going to plays, lighting bonfires, or electing a Pope of Fools and parading him through the streets.

A noisy crowd started gathering outside the Palace of Justice before dawn, eager to get good seats for the play to be performed there at noon, when church officials and important guests would arrive. While they waited, the crowd of poor townspeople, rowdy students, and ragged beggars climbed the tall pillars, broke windows, and shouted to the actors and to Pierre Gringoire, the play's young author, for the show to begin.

Fearful that the shouts would lead to a riot, Pierre began the play. But the officials soon began arriving, and an usher in the gallery announced each one by name. These announcements and the spectators' noisy laughter and discussion of each arrival interrupted the play frequently.

These interruptions frustrated the young playwright, but they were nothing compared to the horror he felt when still another interruption came from a visitor from Belgium. The man suddenly rose in the gallery and called down, "People of Paris, I've been waiting for those people on stage to move, to act, to fight, but all these fools do is call each other names. I had hoped to see a Pope of Fools elected. Back home, we have all the candidates stick

The Spectators' Noisy Laughter

their head through a hole and make faces at the audience. The one who makes the ugliest face is elected Pope of Fools. At least, *that's* amusing. This play is certainly not!"

The crowd cheered. "A Pope! Let's elect our Pope of Fools!"

A student knocked a hole in a small, round chapel window, and soon men were pushing to take their turn making faces. There were angry faces, silly faces, animal faces, grotesque faces. There were opened mouths and closed ones, twisted noses and flat ones, hairy foreheads and bald ones. Each new face sent peals of laughter through the crowd.

Then suddenly, a burst of applause and cheers greeted a monstrous face. It had a small left eye half hidden by a bristly red eyebrow and a right eye that was completely closed and covered by an enormous wart. The nose was more like a pyramid than a nose as it sat above thick lips. Jagged teeth stuck out from those lips, with one looking more like an

A Pope of Fools!

elephant's tusk than a tooth. The face wore a look of amazement mixed with malice and sadness.

The vote was unanimous. This was the winning face—the Pope of Fools had been elected!

But when the crowd rushed to congratulate their new pope, they were startled to discover that the twisted face he had shown in the window was actually his natural face. And that twisted face belonged to an even more twisted body. His huge head bristled with stiff red hair that fell behind him onto an enormous hump on his back. One of his legs was shorter than the other. They seemed to meet at the knees, then spread apart before they ended in immense feet, which matched his enormous hands.

None of this seemed to bother the crowd. They dressed him in a red and purple coat covered with little bells and led him around the big hall.

Dressed in a Red and Purple Coat

THE HUNCHBACK OF NOTRE DAME

"It's Quasimodo, the bellringer!" called one ragged man.

"It's the hunchback of Notre Dame!" cheered a student.

"It's one-eyed Quasimodo! Bow-legged Quasimodo!" joined in the rest of the crowd.

"What an ugly ape!" exclaimed one woman.

"It must be the devil himself!" cried another. "I've seen him casting spells on people from his balcony at Notre Dame."

The visitor from Belgium came down from the gallery, full of wonder. "By God!" he exclaimed to Quasimodo. 'You have the finest ugliness I've ever seen in my entire life."

When Quasimodo didn't answer, the man patted him on the shoulder. "What's the matter, my good fellow, are you deaf?"

Actually, the hunchback *was* deaf and he was also becoming annoyed at the stranger. He suddenly turned on him with a snarl that made the man jump back in fear and surprise.

Turning on Him With a Snarl

THE HUNCHBACK OF NOTRE DAME

An old woman explained to the stranger, "Quasimodo *is* deaf, but he can talk when he wants to. He lost his hearing from ringing the bells at Notre Dame. But he's not dumb."

Just then, a group of ragged beggars surrounded the hunchback and placed a cardboard crown on his head, a ragged robe around his shoulders, and an old wooden stick painted to look like a bishop's staff in his hands.

The newly crowned Pope of Fools was then seated on a litter. Twelve men, serving as the Army of Fools, lifted the litter onto their shoulders and led the boisterous, screaming procession out of the hall and into the streets of Paris.

Looking down from his litter at the heads of the strong, well-built men carrying him was the deformed hunchback. His face was now beaming with joy. He was proud! He was important! He was special! He was the Pope of Fools!

Into the Streets of Paris

Disappointed Over His Failed Play

CHAPTER 2

The Gypsy Girl

Pierre Gringoire stayed in the deserted hall for several hours, disappointed over his failed play. He had nowhere to go, for he had been thrown out of his tiny room for not having paid rent in six months.

When he finally did leave the hall, it was evening. He looked down the street towards the Place de Gréve in the distance. The glow of the festival's bonfires lit up the darkening sky. "I might as well head there, to the square," he said to himself. "At least I can warm myself at the fires since I have no room to go home to. At any other time, the Place de Gréve wouldn't be a welcome sight for me, since it's one of the favorite gallows and flogging places in all of Paris."

But when he reached the square and saw the crowd around the fire, his disappointment returned. "It looks like I'll never get close enough to warm myself," he moaned.

Still, Pierre pushed his way through the crowd only to see that the men in the circle were too far from the fire to be warming themselves. They had formed a circle around a beautiful young girl dancing in front of the fire. Her bare arms stretched high above her long, black hair, and her dark eyes flashed as she beat her tambourine to keep the rhythm of her dance.

When it was over, the crowd cheered as the breathless girl called to a little white goat that had been lying at the edge of the carpet on which she danced.

The goat came to the center of the carpet and watched as the girl held out her

Her Dark Eyes Flashed.

tambourine. "What month is it, Djali?" she asked.

The goat struck the tambourine one time with its hoof. The crowd applauded, for indeed, it *was* the first month, January.

Then the girl turned the tambourine a different way and asked, "What day of the month is it, Djali?" And the goat raised its hoof and tapped the tambourine six times.

Next, when the girl turned her tambourine and asked the time of day, the goat tapped seven times. The crowd was amazed.

"She's a witch!" cried one angry voice.

Everyone turned to see who had spoken. It was a man about thirty-five years old who was almost totally bald. It was too dark to see his clothing, and no one really cared as they turned back to watch the girl.

"Now, Djali, show us how the churchmen preach." And the goat sat back on its rump, put its front legs together as if in prayer, and turned its head from side to side.

"She's a Witch!"

THE HUNCHBACK OF NOTRE DAME

The crowd laughed and cheered.

"That's a sacrilege, an insult to the church!" cried the bald man.

The gypsy girl gave the man a nasty look, then turned away to take up a collection in her tambourine. When she came to Pierre, he put his hand in his pocket. "It's empty," he whispered sadly. "I'm sorry. I'd give you whatever I had if I had anything, but—"

Just then, a shrill, screeching voice interrupted Pierre's apology. "Go away, you gypsy wench! You creature from hell!" The voice was coming from a small, barred window in a stone building facing the square.

"Don't pay any attention to her," said a student standing beside Pierre. He pointed to an old, gray-haired woman clutching at the bars. "Gudule's a crazy old recluse who cemented herself up in that cell fifteen years ago. She can't get out and doesn't want to. As for gypsies, she hates them all and rages at them whenever they're nearby. She blames them for

"You Creature From Hell!"

kidnapping her baby fifteen years ago. She's a pitiful creature who has been kept alive all these years by kind townspeople who pass food to her through the window. When she's not screaming at gypsies, she talks to her baby's tiny, embroidered shoe, which is all she has left. Sometimes she sounds crazy and other times, sane."

Several students in the crowd had just begun to shout back at the old recluse when the procession carrying the Pope of Fools came winding through the Place de Gréve. It had added hundreds more gypsies, beggars, thieves, and robbers, all with torches.

At the center of the procession was the litter carrying the hunchback. During the journey around Paris, a look of pride had replaced the sadness on his face. Pride was a new feeling for him, since he had known only humiliation and scorn all his life because of his hideous appearance.

Even though the crowd pretended to show

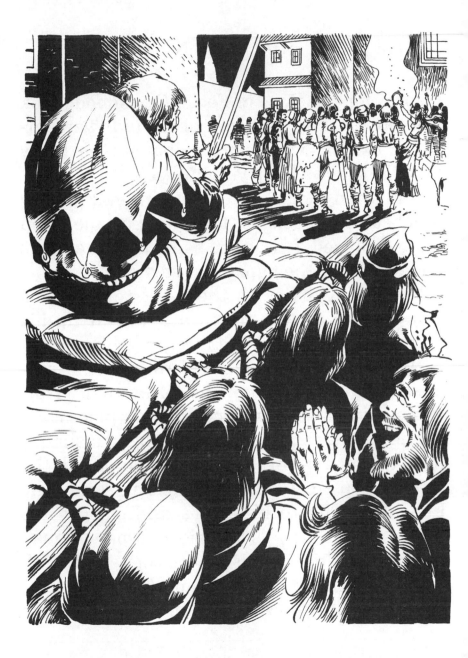

Pride Was a New Feeling for Him.

respect for the Pope of Fools, Quasimodo took it seriously. His confused brain didn't understand exactly what was going on; he knew only that he was enjoying himself.

But when a man ran up to him and angrily grabbed his wooden staff, he became even more confused. It was the same bald man who had cursed at the gypsy girl earlier.

Now, the candles on the litter revealed his church robe for the first time and lit up his face enough for Pierre to recognize him.

"Why, it's Dom Claude Frollo, the Archdeacon of Notre Dame!" he exclaimed. "That one-eyed monster will tear him to pieces!"

The crowd shrieked in terror as Quasimodo leaped down from the litter and faced the priest. But instead of attacking him, the hunchback fell to his knees and clasped his hands in prayer. The priest broke Quasimodo's staff across his knee, then pulled off his crown and robe. Everyone knew that the deaf bell-ringer could have crushed Dom

Clasping His Hands in Prayer

Claude with his bare hands, but he just knelt there silently while the priest made angry, threatening gestures to him.

Finally, Dom Claude shook Quasimodo's shoulder and motioned for him to stand up and follow him. The hunchback obeyed.

The Army of Fools stood ready to defend their Pope and began to follow the two men out of the square. Suddenly, Quasimodo turned and shook his huge, clenched fists at them. Snarling like an enraged animal, he held back the angry mob, protecting the very man who, only moments before, had just attacked him.

"Amazing!" exclaimed Pierre Gringoire, watching in astonishment. "A hunchback, a gypsy girl, and an archdeacon. What perfect subjects for me to write a play about! But for now, I'd better worry about how to fill my stomach with food before I worry about filling a paper with words!"

"What Perfect Subjects for a Play!"

Struggling with Two Men

CHAPTER 3

Two Rescues

When Pierre saw the gypsy girl leave the square, he decided to follow her. "Gypsies are good-hearted people," he told himself. "Perhaps some of them would be willing to share their dinner with me."

The streets were dark as the girl hurried along, with her goat at her side. Just as she turned a corner and was out of sight for a moment, Pierre heard her scream.

He ran to the corner. In a light coming from a lantern in a window, he saw her struggling with two men. He hurried to her rescue, but suddenly found himself face to face with the monstrous form of Quasimodo. A blow from the hunchback's huge hand sent the young poet sprawling, unconscious, to the pavement on the other side of the street.

Quasimodo then bolted off, with the girl under his arm. He was followed by his accomplice, the archdeacon Claude Frollo, and Djali, the goat.

"Murder! Murder!" screamed the girl.

Suddenly, a horseman dashed up from a side street. "Halt, you scoundrels!" he roared as he drew his sword.

The Captain of the King's Archers seized the girl from Quasimodo and threw her across his saddle. Just as the hunchback was about to pull her back, a group of soldiers rode up and surrounded him.

Seeing the hunchback captured, the archdeacon ducked into a darkened doorway, then managed to escape down another side street.

The girl looked up at the handsome young officer. Her eyes shone with admiration as she

"Halt, You Scoundrels!"

asked sweetly, "What's your name, sir?"

The officer proudly replied, "Captain Phoebus de Chéteaupers, at your service."

The girl smiled and slid down from the horse. "Then Esmeralda, the gypsy, thanks you, Captain Phoebus," she said as she watched him ride off down the dark street.

By the time the cold pavement and the wet mud brought Pierre back to his senses, he was alone on the street. He managed to get to his feet and began to stumble along, not knowing where he was going. Finally, a reddish glow at the end of a long, narrow street gave him some hope. "Perhaps that's a fire and I can warm myself. Or perhaps some kind soul is cooking there."

As he made his way along, the street began to fill up with ragged beggars, bandaged blind men and shapeless cripples. When this crowd reached the square, crutches were thrown away and men walked, bandages were removed from eyes that now looked around, and

"Captain Phoebus at Your Service."

missing legs appeared from under the jackets of one-legged beggars.

"Where am I?" gasped Pierre.

"At the Court of Miracles," answered a smiling, toothless beggar in front of him.

Pierre caught his breath. Scattered in the square were tables covered with bottles of wine and mugs of beer. Men and women sat, stood, or leaned on the tables or on each other, singing, laughing, drinking, and even fighting.

"No sane honest man comes here at this hour," Pierre told himself. "Even police have disappeared in this den of robbers, beggars, and murderers!" But his conversation with himself was interrupted when he was suddenly grabbed by three beggars.

"Take him to the king!" shouted one.

"Take him to the king!" echoed the crowd.

Pierre felt himself being dragged towards a large barrel near the fire. Seated on the barrel

"Take Him to the King!"

was a beggar in ragged clothes and a hat resembling a nightcap.

"Here's our king on his throne," announced one of the beggars. "King Clopin."

"Who's this rascal?" demanded the king. "And how dare he enter my kingdom without permission! Is he a thief or a beggar or a gypsy?"

"I'm not any of those, your majesty. I'm a poet," explained Pierre. "I wrote the play that was almost performed this morning at the Palace of Justice—"

"For that, we'll hang you! You bored us this morning, so we'll hang you tonight."

"But, sire, I've committed no crime. You can't sentence me to death without letting me speak!"

"Well, if you want to avoid hanging for a while, you can do so by becoming an outlaw like us."

Pierre eagerly agreed. "I'll be an outlaw, a thief, a beggar, or anything else you want me to be."

King Clopin

THE HUNCHBACK OF NOTRE DAME

"That's fine, but first you'll have to pass a test."

The king signaled to his men, who then brought out a portable gallows with a figure, much like a scarecrow, hanging from it. The dummy was dressed in a red suit covered with hundreds of tiny bells.

Once the men had placed a rickety old stool beneath the swinging dummy, Clopin ordered Pierre, "Stand on it."

"But I'll break my neck," he protested. "One of the legs is broken."

"Stand on it, I said. And hold one of your legs in the air while you balance yourself on the other. Then put your hand inside the dummy's pocket and take out the purse *without* making any of the bells jingle. If you do it, you live. If you fail, you hang!"

The crowd applauded and gathered around the gallows, laughing. Pierre said a silent prayer, then climbed onto the stool, trying to balance himself on one leg as he reached for

"If You Fail, You Hang!"

the dummy. But the wobbly leg on the stool tipped it over, and he lost his balance. As he fell, he grabbed for the dummy, crashing heavily and noisily with it to the ground.

Lying face down on the cold stone, Pierre heard Clopin order, "Pick the rascal up and hang him right away! . . . No, wait! I almost forgot something. It's our custom to ask if any gypsy woman wishes to marry the prisoner. If one does, she can save his life."

Pierre took a deep breath. He still had a chance.

"Well, does anybody here want him?" called Clopin. "Come, ladies, come take a look."

A few women came up to the gallows, but none would marry him, one because he had no money, another because he was too thin, and still another because she already had a husband.

Just as Clopin was about to order the hanging to proceed, the beautiful gypsy dancer made her way through the crowd. "I'll take

"Come, Ladies."

him for my husband," she announced.

The rope was removed from Pierre's neck, and Esmeralda handed him a clay jug. "Take this jug and throw it down on the ground," she told him.

Pierre was puzzled, but he did as he was told. The jug broke into four pieces.

Clopin placed his hands on the foreheads of both young people and spoke in a solemn voice. "Poet, she is your wife. Esmeralda, he is your husband. The jug broke into four pieces, so, according to gypsy law, you will be married for four years."

"You Will Be Married for Four Years."

Her Eyes Flashed in Anger.

CHAPTER 4

A Wedding Night Conversation

"I feel like the hero of a fairy tale," Pierre thought as he sat in a cozy room and looked at the pretty girl who was fussing over her little goat. "She must be madly in love with me to have married me so quickly."

Pierre was so convinced that Esmeralda loved him that he stood up and boldly went to embrace her.

Esmeralda slipped out of his arms and turned on him. Her eyes flashed in anger and her hand clutched a dagger. Her goat, too, seemed ready to attack as it stood in front of its mistress and aimed its horns at the bewildered poet.

"You two aren't very friendly," he said.

"And you're very foolish," she replied.

"But why did you marry me if you're going to attack me with a knife?"

"I did it to save you from hanging."

"Oh, well," said Pierre to himself, "I guess she's not so madly in love with me after all." Then he spoke aloud to his new wife. "Well then, if I'm not to be your husband, I'd like to be your friend, more like a brother. Would that suit you?"

When he saw the gypsy girl smile and put away her dagger, he went on. "And I'd very much like something to eat!"

When the food had been placed before him, Pierre became curious again. "Don't you want to fall in love with a man one day?"

"Oh, yes, but one who can protect me."

Pierre blushed, knowing that he hadn't been able to do that very thing for her earlier

More Like a Brother

that evening. Then he continued, "Why do they call you Esmeralda?"

"I don't know, except perhaps because of this." And she held up a small bag that hung from her neck. It was made of green silk and had a large piece of green glass, an imitation emerald, in the center.

Pierre reached out to touch it, but Esmeralda stepped back. "Don't touch it!" she cried. "It's a charm that could harm you."

"I don't think I believe in that, but tell me more about yourself. Are you French?"

"I don't know. All I do know is that I came to Paris with the gypsies when I was a very little girl. But what about you? I don't even know your name."

"My name is Pierre Gringoire. My parents were killed when I was six and I guess I somehow managed to survive for several years by begging for food and a place to sleep. By the time I was sixteen, I began trying many different professions, but none suited me. Finally

"Don't Touch It!"

THE HUNCHBACK OF NOTRE DAME

I began writing. That's when I was lucky enough to meet Dom Claude Frollo, the Archdeacon of Notre Dame. He taught me languages, mathematics, and science. I owe him a great deal."

"Which profession did you finally follow?"

"I became a poet. I hope one day to make a lot of money from my writing and I'll gladly share it with you."

"Then if you're a man of languages and literature, you must know what words mean."

Pierre nodded modestly.

"Tell me what does the name *Phoebus* mean?"

The young poet was pleased that he could show off some of his knowledge. "It's a Latin word meaning 'sun.' It's also the name of a handsome archer who was a god."

"A god!" she exclaimed, and with a dreamy expression on her beautiful face, she turned and left the room.

"A God!"

"It's a Misshapen Ape!"

CHAPTER 5

The Bellringer of Notre Dame

Outside the Cathedral of Notre Dame was a shelf where orphaned or unwanted children were left to be adopted or raised through public charity. Sixteen years before the celebration of the Festival of Fools just described, a screaming, writhing creature had been left on that shelf. That creature caused unusual interest and curiosity among the crowd of women gathered there.

"This is not a child!" exclaimed one.

"It's a misshapen ape," said another.

"The nurses in the orphanage could hardly nurse this monster!" cried a third.

THE HUNCHBACK OF NOTRE DAME

"This isn't an infant to be nursed; this monster's at least four years old and ready to chew on some meat," decided a fourth.

And it was, indeed, a small, writhing four-year-old whose body was wrapped in a canvas bag, with only its deformed head showing. The head was covered with a mass of red hair, one eye that was closed and the other weeping, a mouth that was screaming, and teeth that looked for something to bite.

"That creature would be better off dead!" cried a woman, storming away in disgust.

Just then, a young priest who had been listening to the conversation pushed his way through the crowd. "I'll adopt this child," he said, lifting him up and wrapping his cassock around him. Then he turned and carried the child into the cloister, the church building where the priests lived.

The crowd watched in bewilderment until one woman finally broke the silence. "Didn't I tell you that that young priest was a sorcerer?

"I'll Adopt This Child!"

THE HUNCHBACK OF NOTRE DAME

Only a sorcerer would adopt such a creature or even go near it."

But Dom Claude Frollo was not a sorcerer at all; he was a young priest whose unusual appearance and strange habits caused gossip among the superstitious people of Paris. His head was almost bald for a man so young, his lips were clenched tightly in bitterness, his dark eyes seemed to flash fire, and he was often seen going into a secret cell he kept in the tower of Notre Dame, a cell that often glowed with a strange red light that was said to be the result of his experiments with alchemy—with turning metals into gold. All these things contributed to the accusations of sorcery.

Actually, Dom Claude was a brilliant young nobleman whose parents had died during a plague when he was nineteen. From that day on, he had devoted himself to the church and then to the deformed child he adopted.

His Dark Eyes Flashed Fire!

THE HUNCHBACK OF NOTRE DAME

It wasn't until Dom Claude took the child out of the canvas bag that he realized just how deformed he actually was. His head was sunk down between his shoulders, his back was arched in a hump, and his legs were twisted. But the more deformed the child was, the more the priest was determined to care for him. He baptized his adopted child and named him Quasimodo, either because he found him on the holiday called Quasimodo Sunday or because the name was made up of two Latin words that meant "partly" and "formed." And Quasimodo *was* partly, or incompletely, formed.

Quasimodo grew up loving the Cathedral of Notre Dame as his home and his school, and almost never left it. He also grew up loving Dom Claude even more, for it was the priest who protected him from the cruelty of other children and who taught him to speak and read and write. Quasimodo's gratitude made him a devoted servant, actually a slave, to the

Loving Dom Claude

priest. And it was Dom Claude who gave him the job of bellringer of Notre Dame when the boy was fourteen and the priest had already been elevated in the church to the position of archdeacon.

However, the sound of the bells broke the boy's eardrums and he became deaf. His deafness then kept him from speaking, for he feared being laughed at even more than he already was. Still, there were times when speaking was absolutely necessary. At those times, Quasimodo found his tongue stiff and awkward. So he communicated with signs and gestures, but only with his master.

To Quasimodo, every inch of every hall and cell and tower and staircase of Notre Dame were as familiar as any child's home would be. He crawled along the outside of the towers like a lizard crawls on walls. He jumped and climbed and swung and played from the bottom of the cathedral to the top, from the inside arches to the huge stone statues

Like a Lizard Crawls on Walls

outside along the Gallery of Kings, and from one monstrous gargoyle to another in the high towers. At times, it was difficult to tell Quasimodo's enormous, deformed head from those of the gargoyles that served as water spouts around the towers.

His deformity also confused his brain and made him malicious to people. But this was understandable, for all his life he had been mocked, insulted, and rejected by everyone.

His greatest love was his bells. He spoke to them, caressed them, and understood them. Their sounds were the only sounds he could still hear. His favorites bells were Big Marie and her sister Jacqueline in the southern tower, though he also cared for and rang thirteen others in the northern tower.

When the archdeacon signaled that it was time for the bells to be rung, Quasimodo would run up the spiral staircase of the tower faster than another person could have run down. Even though he was out of breath when he

His Greatest Love Was His Bells

reached Big Marie, he would gaze at her lovingly for a moment, then talk to her and stroke her. Then he would seize the rope to start the huge metal bell moving.

As the bell gained speed, its great peals caused the whole tower to tremble. This gave Quasimodo such joy that he would run back and forth, following the bell from one side of the tower to the other. Then, as if overcome by a frenzy, his eyes would wildly flash fire and he would leap onto the bell with all his might. He would soar with the bell, clinging to it with his powerful arms, gripping it with his deformed knees, and pushing it with the weight and strength of his entire body. He would shriek at the top of his lungs and gnash his teeth furiously.

It seemed that the bell and the bellringer were no longer two separate things, for they had become one . . . a creature that was half-man and half-bell. A creature that existed only in the strangest nightmare.

Soaring with the Bells

"Quasimodo!"

CHAPTER 6

A Trial and Punishment

The morning after the Festival of Fools, Quasimodo was brought into the courtroom with his hands and arms tied behind him.

The judge looked down at him and coldly announced, "You are accused of creating a disturbance last night, attacking a young woman, and resisting arrest by a captain of the guards. What do you have to say?"

The deaf bellringer assumed that the judge was simply asking his name, so he answered, "Quasimodo."

All the spectators in the courtroom burst out laughing, and the judge cried out in a rage, "How dare you make fun of me!"

"Bellringer of Notre Dame," replied Quasimodo, thinking the judge had asked him his occupation.

"Bellringer! You'll be punished for this!"

"Twenty," said Quasimodo. "I think I'm twenty years old."

That was too much! "I'll teach you to laugh at the Magistrate of Paris!" roared the judge. "I sentence you to be flogged on the pillory at the Place de Gréve for one hour, then turned for another hour."

Quasimodo was dragged out of the courtroom and thrown into a cart for the ride to the Place de Gréve. A crowd had already gathered there, hoping to see a hanging, but ready to be just as amused by a flogging.

Laughter and cheers greeted Quasimodo as the cart stopped in front of the ten-foot-high scaffold. He was led, in a daze, up the rough, stone steps to the platform, where he was

Laughter and Cheers Greeted Quasimodo

shoved to his knees on a large wooden wheel, his hands still tied behind his back.

The guards tore off his shirt, revealing his bare hump and hairy chest, which made the crowd laugh and cheer even more.

When the man known as The Torturer mounted the platform, carrying his famous leather whip knotted with metal spikes, the crowd became silent. He put a large hourglass down on the platform, then signaled the guards to start the wheel turning, to allow all the spectators to see the prisoner on all sides.

When Quasimodo's monstrous back was facing The Torturer, the man raised his arm and brought his whip down furiously across the hunchback's shoulders. Quasimodo jumped in shock, then twisted violently as he finally understood what was happening. But not a sound came from his lips. And not a sound came after the second or third or fourth blow, or after the countless others that followed

Jumping in Shock!

with each turn of the wheel.

The look on the hunchback's face, which at first was one of surprise and shock, soon changed to anger, then rage, then exhaustion. At last, it turned to hopelessness. From that point on, he never moved a muscle.

When the sand in the hourglass had all flowed down, the Torturer stopped his horrible lashes. But Quasimodo's punishment wasn't over. He still had to spend another hour being turned on the wheel, another hour for the townspeople to taunt him, to have them take vengeance against a man whose only crime was being ugly and deformed.

Although the hunchback was deaf to the crowd's insults and curses, he recognized the fury in their faces and felt the stings of the stones they were hurling at him. For a moment, he opened his one eye and saw a priest riding through the crowd on a mule. A weak smile crossed his face as he believed that his master had finally come to save

Turned on the Wheel

him. But Dom Claude only lowered his eyes and turned his mule away from the pillory, away from the Place de Gréve . . . away from Quasimodo, his son.

Bitterness, sadness, and hopelessness returned to Quasimodo's face and stayed there until the rage and pain became too much for the abused and confused hunchback to bear. He open his eye and, with his tongue hanging out and his mouth foaming, he cried out with the fury of a wild animal, "Water!"

Quasimodo's distress brought only jeers and laughter from the crowd.

"Water!" he cried again, this time even more pitifully.

"Drink this!" called a student, as he threw a muddy rag in the hunchback's face.

"Water, please!" he begged again.

Just then, a gypsy girl pushed her way through the crowd. Quasimodo's eyes sparkled as he recognized the dancing girl he had tried to carry off the night before.

Pushing Her Way Through the Crowd

"Is she coming to take her revenge on me too?" he wondered. And he leaned away from her outstretched hands.

But Esmeralda came up to him and lifted a small gourd filled with water to his parched lips. Quasimodo was so amazed at this act of kindness that a tear trickled down out of his deformed eye and he forgot to drink. The gypsy girl pressed the neck of the gourd up against his lips, and the tortured man drank eagerly in long gulps.

The sight of the beautiful girl's kindness and the pitiful creature's gratitude touched even the hardest heart in the crowd. Only one voice, that of the old recluse at the barred window, denounced Esmeralda's act of kindness.

"Curse you, gypsy girl! You'll be up on that pillory or on those gallows some day! And I'll be here to watch and laugh!"

When Quasimodo's turning on the wheel was over and he was set free, the crowd lost interest in him and left the Place de Gréve.

A Tear Trickled from His Eye

Standing on the Balcony

CHAPTER 7

Esmeralda's Admirers

Several weeks later, on a beautiful March morning, Captain Phoebus de Cháteaupers was standing with his fiancée, Fleur-de-Lys de Gondelaurier, on the balcony of her mansion overlooking the square at Notre Dame. The handsome officer looked bored with the pretty young woman beside him, and the idea of marrying her was becoming more and more disagreeable to him. He much preferred spending this time drinking in the tavern and enjoying himself with the women he met there.

"Look down in the square, Phoebus!" said

THE HUNCHBACK OF NOTRE DAME

Fleur-de-Lys. "Isn't that dancer with the little white goat the same gypsy girl you told me you rescued from some bandits?"

"Yes, I think it is. And we're not the only ones watching her. Look across the square, on the top tower of Notre Dame. That man in black looks like the archdeacon."

"Why would *he* be watching? I've heard he doesn't like gypsies. And that's a shame, for she's a wonderful dancer. Phoebus, since you know her, ask her to come dance for us."

"She probably wouldn't remember me, but I'll try . . . Mademoiselle," he called down.

Esmeralda looked up. A joyous smile spread over her face at the sight of the handsome captain beckoning to her. She stopped dancing and walked toward the mansion.

"Come in, my girl," said Phoebus when a servant led Esmeralda to the door of the balcony room. "I don't know if you recog—"

"Oh, yes!" she exclaimed, her eyes shining. "I couldn't forget you. You rescued me."

"You Rescued Me!"

"Yes, from a wicked-looking, one-eyed hunchback. But he got his punishment on the pillory the next day, so I hear. What in the world did he want with you, my pretty one?"

Fleur-de-Lys was not at all pleased with Phoebus's admiring looks at the gypsy girl, so, to embarrass the girl she made fun of her appearance. "You're a disgrace, wearing such a short skirt and with your arms bare!"

A flash of anger crossed Esmeralda's face, but she was more interested in the happiness she was feeling as she stared at Phoebus.

"Don't pay any attention to Fleur-de-Lys," said the captain, laughing. "Clothes don't matter to a pretty girl like you."

"Is she a pretty girl or a witch?" snapped Fleur-de-Lys. "I'm told that gypsies with goats are witches and have taught their animals to do miraculous things. Suppose you show us a miracle, gypsy girl."

"My name is Esmeralda and I'm *not* a witch. And Djali doesn't perform miracles, only tricks

"You're a Disgrace!"

I've taught her." With that, the girl turned on her heels and headed for the door.

"No, wait," said Phoebus, hurrying after her. "Please stay and dance. *I* want you to." Then he whispered something into her ear.

Meanwhile, Fleur-de-Lys had lured the goat to her side with a biscuit and was opening a small cloth bag hanging around Djali's neck. Out tumbled little squares of wood, each containing a letter of the alphabet.

The goat then used its hoof to arrange certain letters in a certain order, a trick Esmeralda had trained it to do.

Fleur-de-Lys jumped back, shuddering. "She *is* a witch!" she cried. "Look what the goat spelled out—PHOEBUS." And the young woman fell to the floor in a faint.

Phoebus went to catch her, but his eyes were fixed on Esmeralda, who was picking up Djali's alphabet squares. The vain man was delighted that the girl was so interested in him that she taught her goat to spell his

The Goat Spelled Out — PHOEBUS

name, that he regretted seeing her leave.

Meanwhile, in the square, Pierre Gringoire had been entertaining the spectators by balancing a chair between his teeth. But his act was interrupted by the arrival of Dom Claude angrily pushing through the crowd.

The archdeacon, who had been looking down at Esmeralda from the cathedral tower for several hours, had become enraged when he saw a man holding her goat. "She's always been alone when she danced," he stormed. "Who's that man with her now?" And he came running down to the square to find out.

"Where is she?" demanded Dom Claude when he reached the young performer. "And who are . . . good heavens! It's you, Master Pierre."

Pierre's concentration was broken and the chair came tumbling down. Hanging his head in embarrassment, he admitted, "I'm ashamed to admit, sir, that a poet such as I must be using my talent this way. But alas! My writing

Balancing a Chair Between His Teeth

has not filled my stomach with bread and my balancing tricks have. A man must earn a living for himself and his wife."

"Wife? I didn't know you had married."

"Yes, the gypsy dancer is my wife."

"How could you!" screamed the archdeacon. "You wretched scoundrel! Marrying a gypsy is against the laws of the church." But that was only an excuse to hide his jealousy.

"Well, actually, it's not a real marriage. I broke the gypsy jug into four pieces and we're only married for four years. We're really friends, more like brother and sister than husband and wife. You see, Esmeralda is very superstitious. She believes that the charm she wears around her neck in a little bag has the power to lead her to her real parents. She's convinced that if she marries anyone, the charm will lose its power. That idea is so firmly fixed in her head that nothing and no one can get it out."

Pierre's explanation calmed Dom Claude,

"The Gypsy Dancer is My Wife."

but the archdeacon was determined to rid Esmeralda of that superstition . . . for his own sake and for his own reasons!

Pierre went on. "Because of her kindness, her gaiety, and her lively manner, she's very popular with her gypsy friends, and they'll do anything to protect her. In all of Paris, there's no one who doesn't love her for those qualities, except perhaps two people she says hate her, two people she fears. One is the old recluse in the barred cell who screams out at her when she dances, and the other is some priest who stares at her and follows her and speaks frightening words to her. But tell me, Dom Claude, why are you so interested in Esmeralda?"

"I-I'm interested only in *you* and your welfare, Master Pierre," stammered the archdeacon, trying to cover his lies.

Then fearing that his nervousness and red face would give him away, Dom Claude turned and hurried back into the cathedral, leaving Pierre standing in the square, puzzled.

Hurrying Back

"I Can't Stand that Woman!"

CHAPTER 8

The "Murder" of Captain Phoebus

A while later, after Esmeralda and Pierre had finished performing and the crowd had scattered, the archdeacon came out of the cathedral into the deserted square. He was still seething from his talk with the young poet. As he headed across the square, he saw an officer leave the Gondelaurier mansion and greet an aide waiting for him outside.

"By God, I can't stand that woman in there!" cried Captain Phoebus de Chateaupers, pointing back to the house. "Not only is she boring me, but she's driving me crazy as well! If she weren't so rich, I'd—"

"But, Captain, she's your fiancée."

"I think I need a drink to forget that. Besides, I have other plans for tonight . . . plans with that beautiful gypsy girl who was dancing in the street today." Then he whispered something to his aide, and they both began to laugh loudly.

"Are you sure she'll meet you?"

"Of course! She'll be there at seven."

"Captain Phoebus, you're a lucky man!"

The archdeacon began trembling with rage when he heard this conversation. "I must stop him! He must never lay a hand on her!" he gasped. And as the two laughing men left the dark square, he began to follow them.

After several blocks, the officers entered a tavern. Dom Claude waited and watched from a dark doorway across the street, stamping his feet to keep warm in the cold night air.

Finally, two drinkers stumbled out, their arms on each other's shoulders, their voices

Whispering Something

raised in a loud drinking song.

"Our pockets are empty, but our stomachs are certainly filled with wine," babbled the captain as he staggered from side to side. "And now my gypsy girl is waiting for me."

Phoebus waved his sword in farewell to his aide before turning down a dark deserted side street. Dom Claude followed, creeping softly as the captain stumbled along, stopping when he stopped to lean against a wall.

But Phoebus was a brave soldier and when he noticed he was being followed, he suddenly stopped and stood motionless against a statue built into a stone wall. "Now I'll see what this shadow wants," he thought. Then he forced a loud laugh and called, "Sir, if you're a robber, you're wasting your time. My pockets are empty."

A strong hand reached out and grabbed Phoebus's arm, and a cold voice demanded, "Captain Phoebus de Cháteaupers!"

"How do you know my name?"

A Strong Hand Reached Out

"Your name isn't all I know," said the eerie voice. "I know you have an appointment tonight at seven o'clock with a woman."

"That's right," said Phoebus in amazement.

"And her name is—"

By now, Phoebus's head was clearing from the wine, and he was feeling carefree and confident again. "Her name is Esmeralda, the gypsy girl," he boasted.

"You're lying!"

"How dare you insult me by calling me a liar! Draw your sword and prepare to die!"

"You wish to fight instead of keeping your appointment?" sneered the archdeacon. Then seeing the officer lower his sword, he went on. "Since you have no money and you'll need some to buy wine for the lady, take this." He slipped a coin into the officer's hand, then continued. "You can prove me wrong by letting me follow you and see if the woman is really the one you say."

"Her Name is Esmeralda."

"That's fine with me, my generous friend," said Phoebus, seeing the gold coin clutched in his hand. "Come along then."

The two men walked along a dark street that ended at the river. When they reached the last house, Phoebus pounded on a low door. An old ragged woman opened it and led the men up a dark staircase.

Even in the blackness, Dom Claude kept his cloak pulled up around his eyes so as not to be recognized. And he stayed behind Phoebus as they approached an open door.

"Oh, Captain Phoebus, you've come at last!" cried Esmeralda, jumping up from a bench where she had been seated, with Djali at her feet. "You're so kind and so handsome. You were so brave when you rescued me. How can you even look at a poor gypsy girl like me?"

"But you're so beautiful, my dear Similar, I mean Esmenarda—I can never get your outlandish name straight in my mind. But names aren't important now. What *is* important is

"Captain Phoebus, You've Come At Last!"

that you're here and you love me."

"Oh, I do, I do," said the poor girl. "And I'll love you forever. Even though I know that when I marry you, the charm around my neck will lose the power to lead me to my real parents, it doesn't matter any more. I love you and will marry—"

"Marriage isn't important if people love each other," said Phoebus as he reached out to take Esmeralda in his arms. He had no idea what she was talking about when she rambled on about a charm. "Charms aren't important either when two people love each other, and I've never loved anyone but you, my dear, sweet Similar."

These were false words of love Phoebus had spoken many times to many women, but Esmeralda was so trusting that she believed them. She threw her arms around his neck and gazed up at him blissfully. Then she closed her eyes and let him kiss her.

Watching another man kiss Esmeralda

False Words of Love

inflamed the archdeacon's jealousy. He pulled a dagger from his belt and rushed into the room.

As Esmeralda opened her eyes after Phoebus's kiss, she froze in terror, for above his head was a savage, twisted face and a hand that clutched a dagger. Before Esmeralda could cry out, the dagger plunged down into his back. He let out a terrible scream, then he slumped to the floor.

Esmeralda felt everything turn black as she collapsed in a faint beside him.

Some time later, when she recovered consciousness and looked around, the gypsy girl saw the room crowded with soldiers. The window was open and the stranger with the dagger had disappeared.

Two of the soldiers were kneeling over the bloody body of Phoebus de Cháteaupers, while another pointed an accusing finger at Esmeralda. "She's the witch who just stabbed the captain!" he cried.

A Savage, Twisted Face!

"What's Happening?"

CHAPTER 9

A Confession and a Sentence

Everyone in the Court of Miracles was worried. Esmeralda and Djali had been missing for over a month, and searches all over the city had turned up nothing.

Pierre Gringoire's life hadn't changed much even though Esmeralda was gone. Actually, he missed the goat more than he missed his wife! But he went on performing his balancing act to earn a little money.

One day, after finishing his act outside the Palace of Justice, he saw the crowd all streaming inside the building. "What's happening?" he asked an old man.

THE HUNCHBACK OF NOTRE DAME

"A young woman's on trial for murdering an officer. They say she's a witch."

With nothing else to do, Pierre joined the crowd at the back of the large dark courtroom. The prisoner had her back to the crowd and armed guards surrounded her, so Pierre couldn't see or recognize her.

An old woman in the witness box was testifying about renting a room to an officer for a meeting with a gypsy girl. "He came to my house that night with a man in black. They both went upstairs to meet the girl. Then, a while later, I heard someone cry out and something fall to the floor. A moment later, I heard their window being opened. From my own window below, I saw something black fly past and jump into the river. I'd swear it was a ghost dressed up like a priest!"

Gasps were heard among the spectators, but the woman didn't stop. She was enjoying the attention she was getting, so she went on to describe the bloody scene she found when

Gasps Were Heard!

she went upstairs and how she ran to get help. Then she swore, "I'm sure that gypsy girl's a witch who cast a spell over that handsome young officer. And her goat helped too!"

The judge turned to the prisoner. "Well, what have you to say? Did you murder Captain Phoebus de Cháteaupers?"

The pale, frightened, disheveled prisoner stood up. "I'm innocent!" she cried.

At the back of the room, Pierre gasped in horror as he recognized Esmeralda.

But the tearful girl was pleading with the judge. "Where is Phoebus? What has become of him? Please tell me if he's still alive!"

"That's no concern of yours," replied the judge coldly. "But if you must know, I've been told he's dead." Then he turned to a guard and ordered, "Bring in the other prisoner, the one to be tried for witchcraft."

All eyes turned to the door as the guard led Djali into the courtroom. Pierre broke out into a cold sweat, for while he was fond of

"Did You Murder Captain Phoebus?"

Esmeralda, he was fonder of her goat. And in those days, animals were hung as witches, just as people were. He panicked even more when a court official picked up Esmeralda's tambourine, held it in different positions, and asked the goat some questions, just as the gypsy girl used to do.

Then the official emptied Djali's bag of letters onto the floor and the goat spelled out the name PHOEBUS.

The judge was convinced of both prisoners' guilt, but he was required to ask Esmeralda, "Prisoner, on the night of March 29, did you use your powers of witchcraft and, along with this bewitched goat, stab and kill Captain Phoebus de Cháteaupers?"

"I deny everything!" cried Esmeralda. "It was that horrible priest who did it, the same one who's been following me and—"

"Silence!" cried the judge. "Since the prisoner refuses to admit her guilt, I order her to be tortured until she does."

Spelling Out Phoebus

THE HUNCHBACK OF NOTRE DAME

Esmeralda was dragged out of the courtroom and taken down into a cold dark dungeon. Many instruments of torture were scattered about the room, and some were glowing red hot inside a furnace, ready to make a prisoner confess. Even though Esmeralda had no idea how these instruments were used, they frightened her all the same, and she closed her eyes tightly, unable to look at them.

When a guard pushed her into a chair and tied her hands to a strap hanging down from the ceiling, she forced herself to open her eyes again. The guard was lifting her leg and placing it inside a frightful iron boot.

Although the girl began to weep and plead for mercy, the guard tightened the screw that pressed the two halves of the iron boot together. Soon, the boot was crushing her leg, tighter and tighter. When she couldn't bear the pain any longer, Esmeralda uttered a terrible shriek that didn't sound human.

Esmeralda was Dragged Out of the Courtroom.

THE HUNCHBACK OF NOTRE DAME

"Stop! I'll confess. I'll confess to anything. Just put me to death! Without my Phoebus, I don't want to live."

The guards unfastened the boot and dragged the limp gypsy girl back to the courtroom.

The judge announced, "Gypsy girl, you have confessed to all charges of witchcraft and murder. For now, you will be held in a dungeon until a day chosen by the king. Then you will be taken to the front door of the Cathedral of Notre Dame to publicly ask for forgiveness for your sins. After that, you will be taken to the Place de Gréve, where you will be hanged from the gallows. Your goat will be hanged too."

"One day is the same as another. Just kill me quickly," sobbed Esmeralda, as the guards dragged her away.

Her dungeon was a deep, dark hole below the stone walls of the Palace of Justice. No air or light or sound reached down into that hole,

"Just Kill Me Quickly."

only a trap door in the ceiling and a few steps leading down from it.

Esmeralda lay on a small pile of straw, chained by her ankles to the cold wet wall, almost too numb to even breathe. All she could think of were Phoebus's words of love, the priest, the dagger, the murder! It was a horrible nightmare that was always with her.

She didn't know when day became night or how many of each passed. She soon stopped listening for the trap door to open as the jailer dropped a piece of bread and a jug of water down to her once a day.

Then, one day or one night—she had no way of knowing, the trap door opened and a man in a black cloak came down the stone steps. He held a lantern low, near his feet.

"Who are you?" Esmeralda whispered.

"A priest," came a muffled answer. "You are to be hanged tomorrow. Are you ready?"

"Why can't they do it today? I'm so cold and so afraid, and there are animals in here that

"A Priest."

crawl all over my body." She burst into tears like a lost child.

"Then follow me," said the priest, pushing back his hood and revealing his face to her.

"You!" she gasped. "You, the mysterious man who has been following me and terrifying me for months! You, the priest who murdered my beloved Phoebus! What have I done to you that you hate me so?"

"I don't hate you. I love you!"

"What kind of love makes a man so cruel?" she cried. "Especially a priest?"

"Listen and I'll explain," he said calmly. "I'll tell you things I haven't admitted to myself. Before I first saw you dancing in the square, I was a happy man and a good priest. Other priests looked up to me and followed my examples in life. No woman had ever tempted me away from my devotion to God until I became fascinated with you. Then when I saw a goat with you, I knew you were a witch, for witches always use goats in their rituals. I

"I Love You."

became convinced that the devil had sent you to lure me away from God. And I still believe that."

"Then why are you here?"

"Don't interrupt me. I've tried for months to forget you, but I hear your voice singing and see your feet dancing even when you're not in the square. I'm so bewitched that I've been watching you from the towers at the Cathedral, from dark doorways, from street corners. I even tried carrying you off, with the help of a friend, But then that cursed officer rescued you."

"Oh, my Phoebus!"

"Don't even speak the name of that hateful man! He's ruined both of us! He didn't love you or even care about you. He was merely playing with your heart as he did with every woman, while *I* truly love you. But because I'm a priest, I'm not allowed to love you the way I do. So I've been truly miserable. Please, I beg you, have pity on me!"

"Have Pity on Me."

THE HUNCHBACK OF NOTRE DAME

Dom Claude threw himself at Esmeralda's feet. "I beg you, don't turn away from me. I can help you escape. I can't bear seeing you go to the gallows tomorrow. We can run away together and I'll spend my life making you happy." He grabbed her arm frantically and tried to pull her toward him.

"Happy?" cried Esmeralda with a terrible burst of laughter, shaking her arm free of the priest's grip. "Happy when your hand is still bloody from the dagger you stabbed my beloved with! . . . No, murderer, leave me! Let me die! With Phoebus dead, I no longer wish to live. Nothing you can say or do will ever make me pity you. And nothing will ever make me go with you! I'd rather die first!"

Esmeralda began to beat at the priest with her fists. Then, weak and exhausted, she fell back on her pile of straw, sobbing.

Dom Claude picked up his lantern and silently climbed the staircase, slamming the trap door on the girl's pitiful sobs!

"I'd Rather Die First!"

Worshipping Her Shoe

CHAPTER 10

Sanctuary!

It was a sunny May morning when the sounds of horses and wheels and clanking iron broke the silence in the Place de Greve. The old recluse was annoyed by the noise, for it interrupted her worshipping of the tiny shoe that had belonged to her kidnapped baby daughter. She had been spending most of her waking hours grieving over the child and worshiping her shoe for fifteen years. Now she tied her long gray hair over her ears to try to block out the noises.

Her loud wails reached passersby as they headed toward the square. "Oh, my little girl!

THE HUNCHBACK OF NOTRE DAME

I'll never see you again! Oh, God, give her back to me, even if it's for one day or one hour or one minute! I've prayed to you, God, for fifteen years. Isn't that enough?"

The poor woman clutched the little embroidered shoe to her breast and sobbed wildly. It was only the voices of some children outside that stopped her sobbing, for she heard one say, "They're going to hang the gypsy girl today."

She rushed to her barred window and saw the hangman adjusting the chains on the gallows. Standing near her window, also watching the hangman, was a priest. Recognizing him as the archdeacon, she called out, "Father, I hear they're hanging a gypsy girl today." And she began to laugh hysterically.

"Yes, they are, Gudule," he answered. "And I hear you hate all gypsies."

"Every one of them! They're witches, child stealers! And there's one I hate more than the others. She's the one who dances in the

"I Hear You Hate All Gypsies."

street—the young, dark-haired one. She's the same age my daughter would have been if those gypsies hadn't stolen her away from me and killed her."

"Well, then, sister, you can rejoice," said the archdeacon coldly, "for she's the very one you're about to see hanged." And he sadly and slowly walked away.

The recluse threw her hands up to heaven. "Thank You, God!" she cried joyously. Then she began to run around her cell, throwing her body against the stone walls, tearing at her hair, and laughing hysterically.

Meanwhile, a crowd was gathering in the square outside Notre Dame. Word had spread quickly that the gypsy girl was to be hung today and she would first be brought to the church steps for her public confession.

Watching the crowd in the square from her balcony was Fleur-de-Lys Gondelaurier. At her side, with his arms around her, was a handsome soldier.

Waiting for Her Public Confession

THE HUNCHBACK OF NOTRE DAME

"Look, Phoebus," she said as she pointed to the crowd below. "They're all waiting for some prisoner's final confession. I wonder who the prisoner is."

Captain Phoebus de Chateaupers was very much alive on that sunny May morning. While he *had* been wounded by the archdeacon's dagger, he was young and strong and had recovered nicely. Although he had heard about Esmeralda's trial while he was with his troops outside of Paris, he didn't think it was important enough for him to return to the city to testify. He even reasoned that she *was* a witch and that gave him an added reason not to try to save her. Besides, his appearance at the trial might create some problems for him, not only with his superior officers, but with Fleur-de-Lys as well. Marriage to this rich young woman was going to bring him a great deal of money, and he didn't want to risk losing it. And since no one in the Palace of Justice or the church considered it

Captain Phoebus Was Alive.

important enough to check with the doctor to see if he had actually died or recovered, Phoebus kept quiet. He wouldn't be talked about outside the courtroom, and, with no newspapers in Paris at the time, people wouldn't recognize him.

So, now, as he stood with Fleur-de-Lys, he didn't pay too much attention to the crowd or to the soldiers surrounding the cart with the prisoner as it entered the square.

"Here she comes!" shouted the crowd.

The cart that was pulled into the square by a strong horse contained a young girl. Her hands were tied behind her back and a thick rope was wound around her neck. At her feet was a little white goat, also tied up. As the cart jolted her about, she looked like a lifeless rag doll.

"Look, Phoebus!" cried Fleur-de-Lys. "It's the gypsy girl and her goat, the one who—"

Phoebus recognized Esmeralda immediately and turned pale. "W-what g-gypsy girl?" he

"Here She Comes!"

stammered, suddenly frightened that his involvement with the girl would somehow be discovered.

Meanwhile, Esmeralda, terrified and bewildered, was being pulled out of the cart, her eyes lowered and her lips whispering one word over and over, "Phoebus, Phoebus, Phoebus, Phoebus."

Her hands were untied and she was led up the steps of the cathedral. She lifted her eyes as a procession of priests emerged, chanting and holding candles. At the head of the procession was a familiar priest carrying a great golden cross.

"There he is again—that priest!" she whispered to herself.

The archdeacon stared straight ahead as he placed a heavy lighted candle in Esmeralda's hand. Speaking loudly for the crowd to hear, he asked, "Young woman, have you asked God to forgive your sins?" Then he leaned close to her ear, so everyone would

A Procession of Priests Emerged.

think he was hearing her confession, and said, "I can still save you. Will you run away with me?"

"Get away from me, you murderer, or I'll denounce you in front of everyone here!"

"No one would believe you, not one person in this entire crowd." As he said this, his arm swept out towards the crowds in the square and on the balconies around it. "Good Lord!" he gasped as he recognized Phoebus on one balcony. The archdeacon's face twisted in a rage, and he snarled between his teeth so that only Esmeralda could hear him. "All right then, die!"

The priests standing behind him heard none of this conversation and, at a signal from the archdeacon, they chanted, "God have mercy on us" as the crowd knelt in prayer.

As the archdeacon turned away from the girl, two of the guards tied her hands again and led her back to the cart. She was about to climb in when she lifted her eyes to heaven, as

"Good Lord!"

if taking her last look at everything she knew in life. Her eyes traveled down to the rooftops, to the houses, to the balconies . . . and they stopped. She uttered a cry of joy. "My Phoebus! You're alive! The judge lied! The priest lied!"

Esmeralda tried to reach out to him, but her hands were tied. She saw him frown at her, then lead the young woman back into the house, closing the balcony door behind him.

"He thinks I tried to kill him," she whispered. "That's why he turned away from me."

This final blow was too much for Esmeralda to bear. She collapsed on the pavement, and the guards bent down to lift her back into the cart.

All eyes were on the prisoner, so no one noticed a strange spectator leaning over the balustrade, or railing, of Notre Dame's Gallery of the Kings, just above the high center doorway. If it weren't for his red and purple clothing, he might have been mistaken for one of the monstrous stone gargoyles that had been

The Final Blow

sitting there for six hundred years. In his hand, Quasimodo held a long, thick rope that he had tied to one of the huge stone columns.

As the guards were about to pick up the unconscious girl, Quasimodo climbed over the balustrade. Clutching onto the rope with his hands and knees and feet, he slid down the front of the cathedral. No sooner had his feet hit the ground than his fists swung at the guards and knocked them down. He quickly scooped up Esmeralda in his arms and, holding her over his head, rushed into Notre Dame, shouting, "Sanctuary! Sanctuary!"

"Sanctuary! Sanctuary!" repeated the thousands of voices in the crowd.

The guards froze in their tracks. They and the crowd knew that Notre Dame was a sanctuary—a place of refuge, or protection, where no soldier was allowed to enter to make an arrest or take anyone prisoner.

Quasimodo stopped in the great doorway, still holding the unconscious girl in his strong

"Sanctuary! Sanctuary!"

but gentle hands. He hugged her to his bony chest and his deformed eye gazed down at her tenderly.

The women in the crowd laughed and wept at this display of affection, while the men stamped their feet and cheered his bravery. As for the hunchback, he felt proud. He was being cheered by the very same people who had always made him an outcast.

After several minutes of listening to the cheers, Quasimodo turned and hurried into the darkness of the church. Moments later, he appeared on the gallery, with the girl again above his head, and he ran across it, shouting wildly, "Sanctuary!"

He disappeared inside, only to reappear at the top bell tower. From there, he showed the girl to the entire city of Paris as he thundered, "Sanctuary! Sanctuary!"

At the Top of the Bell Tower

Uttering Strange, Gasping Sounds

CHAPTER 11

Gratitude or Pity?

When Esmeralda regained consciousness, she found herself on the floor of a small room high in one of the church towers. Its one tiny window opened onto the stone gargoyles that overlooked the city of Paris.

Bending over her was the deformed face of the hunchback, uttering strange gasping sounds as his huge hands gently took the thick rope off her neck.

"Why did you rescue me?" she asked.

He looked at her with a puzzled expression, not understanding her words because of his deafness. He simply looked at her sadly and went away.

THE HUNCHBACK OF NOTRE DAME

When he returned a while later, he was carrying a mattress under one arm and a basket of food under the other. "Eat and sleep," he said. What he placed on the floor was his own bed and his own meal.

Esmeralda looked up at him to thank him, but the sight of the monstrous creature made her lower her eyes and shudder.

"I frighten you, don't I?" he said. "I know I'm very ugly. But you don't have to look at me, just listen. Stay up here during the day. At night, you can go anywhere in the church. But don't ever leave it, not any time. If they catch you outside this sanctuary, they'll kill you. If anything ever happened to you, I'd want to die too."

Esmeralda was touched by his words, and she forced herself to lift her eyes. It was then that she saw what else the hunchback had brought her.

"Oh, Djali!" she cried, hugging her little goat and sobbing into its soft fur.

"I Frighten You, Don't I?"

"I found your goat wandering outside the church," explained Quasimodo. "I thought it would keep you from being too lonely."

The gypsy girl was so busy hugging and sobbing that she never heard Quasimodo leave the room. She didn't see him again until the following morning when the sun streaming into her cell wakened her. It had been such a long time since she had opened her eyes and seen sunshine that she squinted at the window.

But when her eyes were clear, she saw Quasimodo's monstrous, one-eyed face peering in at her from the window. She gasped in surprise.

"Don't be afraid of me," he said gently. "I'm your friend. I only want to watch you while you're sleeping. That way, your eyes are closed and you don't have to see me. But now that you're up, I'll go away." And he turned and walked away from the window.

"Oh, Djali!"

THE HUNCHBACK OF NOTRE DAME

Esmeralda ran from her room and out onto the gallery. The poor hunchback was crouching in a corner, trying to hide his ugly body beside a grotesque gargoyle.

"Please don't run away," she said with a smile as she touched his arm. "Please come back."

Her smile and her touch brought a look of joy and tenderness to Quasimodo's face. "I-I'm sorry," he stammered, "but I'm deaf and I can't hear your words. It's horrible, I know. You're so beautiful and I'm a miserable monster. But I can understand you if you talk with signs and if I watch your lips. I have a master who talks to me that way."

"Then I'd like to know why you rescued me," she said, facing him as she formed her words and made signs with her hands.

"You've probably forgotten the wretched creature who tried to kidnap you one night. It's the same wretched creature you took pity on the next day and gave water to on the pillory.

Making Signs with Her Hands

You may have forgotten, but I haven't. I'm that creature. And I want you to know that I'd gladly give my life for you. I'd jump from this tower if you wanted me to."

"No, no, don't say such a thing," pleaded Esmeralda. "I'm grateful to you. Please stay with me."

"I can't stay. You're saying that only because you pity me. But that's all right. I just want you to know I'm here to protect you. If ever you need me, at any time day or night, blow on this." He handed her a small metal whistle and explained, "That's one sound I *can* hear."

"I will . . . and thank you."

"Blow on This."

A Glow Returned to Her Eyes

CHAPTER 12

Waiting for Phoebus

As the days passed, the horror of her ordeal slowly began to leave Esmeralda: her trial, her torture, her weeks in the dungeon, even thoughts of the priest himself. A glow returned to her eyes as she filled her thoughts with Phoebus. He was alive and she loved him more than ever.

"Somehow I must see him," she told herself. "I must convince him that it wasn't my dagger that stabbed him. I know he loves me too and he'll come back to me once he knows. As for that woman he stood on the balcony with, I'm certain she must be his sister. After all, he did swear he didn't love any other woman. He swore he loved only me."

Even though Esmeralda was fooling herself by believing Phoebus's lies, they gave her peace and hope and joy.

Quasimodo brought her food each day, but didn't stay to upset her with his ugliness. When he saw her hugging and petting Djali, which she did so often, he regretted his deformity even more. "I'm too ugly to be a man and even too ugly to be an animal. No one will ever hug me or touch me like that!"

And he would spend hours out on the gallery, rubbing his misshapen head against his favorite gargoyle, tearfully pleading, "Why didn't God make me out of stone like you? If only He had, I wouldn't have feelings!"

One morning, Quasimodo was standing behind Esmeralda on the roof. She was at the edge, looking out across the square, when she suddenly gasped and cried out, "It's Phoebus! I see him! Oh, Phoebus, come to me!"

"It's Phoebus."

THE HUNCHBACK OF NOTRE DAME

Quasimodo couldn't hear her words, but he saw her excited face. He hurried over to the edge and looked out across the square. The captain was riding toward the Gondelaurier mansion, waving his plumed helmet at a beautiful woman on the balcony. He was too far away to hear Esmeralda calling him, but the poor, deaf hunchback understood what her cries meant. He heaved a deep sigh and began to beat at his head, tearing out clumps of red hair in anger and frustration.

"He can't hear me," sobbed Esmeralda. "He's going into that house . . . to that woman . . . Phoebus! Phoebus!" She fell to her knees and began to weep uncontrollably.

Quasimodo couldn't bear to see her so unhappy. He tugged at her sleeve and asked, "Would you like me to bring him to you?"

"Oh, yes!" she exclaimed, hugging his knees in gratitude. "Hurry! I'll love you for it!"

Quasimodo rushed down the stairs, shaking his head in sorrow and sobbing as if his heart

Weeping Uncontrollably

were breaking. By the time he crossed the square, only Phoebus's horse was there, tied to a post. The captain had already gone inside, so Quasimodo waited in a nearby doorway. It wasn't until many hours later that Phoebus came out.

"Captain! Captain!" called Quasimodo, grabbing the bridle as Phoebus was mounting his horse. "A woman is waiting for you, a woman who loves you."

"Let go of my horse, you ugly scarecrow!" snapped Phoebus angrily. "If it's a woman as ugly as you, don't bother me. Besides, I'm getting married."

Quasimodo's deafness prevented him from understanding Phoebus, and he thought the captain was asking who the woman was. "It's the gypsy girl, sir. Please come with me."

Phoebus had no way of knowing that Esmeralda was still alive, for on the day of her scheduled execution he had left the balcony with Fleur-de-Lys moments before Quasimodo

"You Ugly Scarecrow!"

rescued her. "The gypsy girl?" he cried as he reached for his dagger. "She's dead! Has she sent you to haunt me?"

Quasimodo began to pull harder on the bridle. But Phoebus kicked him violently in the chest and knocked him to the pavement. Then he galloped off, laughing wickedly.

"Foolish man!" whispered Quasimodo sadly as he got to his feet. "To have someone like *her* love you and to reject her!"

He trudged back to Notre Dame and climbed up to the tower. Esmeralda was still standing in the same spot where he had left her hours earlier. He couldn't bear to repeat Phoebus's cruel words, so he simply said, "I couldn't find him."

Esmeralda's disappointment quickly changed to anger and she snapped, "You should have waited all night!"

"I'll try harder next time," he promised.

"Go away and leave me alone!"

Quasimodo hurried off to his quiet place to

Laughing Wickedly

talk to his favorite gargoyle. "I did the right thing, didn't I? It's better to have her angry at me than to cause her pain."

But his tearful question got no answer from his stone companion.

From that day on, Quasimodo didn't come to Esmeralda's room. He left her food outside her door at night while she slept and sometimes added a vase of flowers and once, a cage with birds. Esmeralda didn't seem to notice his absence, for she was spending her days playing with Djali, talking to herself about Phoebus, and watching for him to ride to the mansion across the square.

The hunchback seemed to have vanished, but one night Esmeralda heard a noise outside her room. She opened her door slightly and discovered him sleeping on the stone floor, guarding her door, protecting her with his body and his life.

Sleeping on the Stone Floor

Obsessed Once Again

CHAPTER 13

Swearing Revenge!

After Esmeralda's final rejection of Dom Claude on the steps of Notre Dame, the archdeacon had immediately fled the city in misery. He had hoped that once she was dead, he would be free of his obsession with her. But on his return the following day, he learned of her miraculous rescue.

Obsessed once again, he locked himself in his room and spent his days with his face pressed against his window, watching Esmeralda and her goat up in the tower. But now, he was also watching Quasimodo as he served her devotedly, and Dom Claude's jealousy began tormenting him once again.

"Being jealous of the poet and the captain was bad enough," he told himself, "but being jealous of *that* creature . . ."

Thoughts of Esmeralda and Quasimodo spending time together agonized him constantly. He couldn't eat; he couldn't sleep. Finally, he worked himself up into such a frenzy one night that he bit his pillow to shreds and leaped out of bed. Throwing a cloak over his nightshirt, he rushed out of his room and headed to the church tower.

In her room, Esmeralda was sleeping peacefully, dreaming, as always, of her Phoebus. A noise at her door woke her, and the face she saw rushing at her made her cry out in terror. "The priest! Monster! Murderer!"

Dom Claude tried to take her in his arms. "Please love me," he begged, but she struck him in the face and began to scream.

"Silence!" he ordered.

"Please Love Me!"

THE HUNCHBACK OF NOTRE DAME

Esmeralda's hand reached under her mattress for Quasimodo's whistle. She put it to her lips and blew as hard as she could.

"What's tha—" began the priest. But at that moment, a powerful arm grabbed him and pulled him away from the girl. Even though the room was dark, Dom Claude was able to make out a sword above his head.

"Help! Quasimodo, come quickly!" he called out to his faithful slave, forgetting for the moment that his faithful slave was deaf.

The archdeacon felt himself being flung against the stone wall, then a heavy knee was pressing against his chest. He suddenly recognized that knee and the outline of the body it was attached to. But in the darkness, he had no way of letting Quasimodo know who he was.

Then Dom Claude felt himself being dragged out of the room, and he heard Quasimodo whisper, "She mustn't see any bloodshed."

Flung Against the Stone Wall

THE HUNCHBACK OF NOTRE DAME

Once outside the door, Quasimodo lit a lamp. To his horror, he discovered who the legs belonged to, and he quickly helped the archdeacon to his feet. Dropping to his knees and reaching out his sword to the enraged priest, Quasimodo said, "Master, kill me if you wish."

But Esmeralda was quicker than the archdeacon. She snatched the sword from Quasimodo's hands and, laughing hysterically, she raised it above Claude Frollo's head. "You lying coward!" she cried. "I know Phoebus is alive! You let me believe he was dead, and you let everyone believe I murdered him!"

At that moment, the archdeacon distracted her by kicking Quasimodo to the floor. Then he rushed down the staircase and back to his room, trembling with rage.

Once inside, he turned to the window and swore into the night, "If you won't love me, you won't love anyone. If I can't have you, no one else will! I'll have my revenge if it's the last thing I ever do!"

"You Lying Coward!"

A Familiar Voice

CHAPTER 14

The Battle for Notre Dame

During the months that Esmeralda was locked in the dungeon and then in the tower of Notre Dame, she had had no word from her husband. Pierre had stayed with the gypsies and thieves in the Court of Miracles, earning a little money from his balancing act.

One day, after finishing his act, he felt a hand on his shoulder and heard a familiar voice asking him, "Master Pierre, how are you and the gypsy girl you married?"

Pierre turned around to smile at his old friend, Dom Claude. "I'm not bad, sir. As for my wife, I've been told that Esmeralda has taken sanctuary at Notre Dame. I'm happy about that, although I haven't seen her."

"She saved your life and you haven't even tried to see her!" thundered Dom Claude.

"W-w-well, I—" stammered the young man.

"Well, I have bad news for you. She is to be arrested again tomorrow and hanged."

"But how can that be? She has sanctuary in the church and no one can—"

"Yes, they can, with a special order from the King of France, and it appears that someone *did* request that order."

"What kind of devil would appeal to the king to take the life of a poor gypsy girl?"

The archdeacon turned his face away and didn't answer. Instead, he asked, "Wouldn't you like to do something to save her?"

"I guess so . . . if it doesn't mean putting a noose around my own neck."

"She must get out of Notre Dame before the soldiers come for her!" Dom Claude insisted, then he muttered to himself, "And I must get

Bad News

her away from Quasimodo!"

"But I don't see any way to get her out," protested Pierre.

"I have an idea. You can go into the church and exchange clothes with her. Then she'll come out in your clothes and you'll stay behind in hers."

The poet's face darkened. "And they'll hang me when they find me! No, thank you."

"She saved *your* life, Pierre!"

"Yes, but . . . wait! I have an idea! The thieves and beggars and gypsies in the Court of Miracles are all brave fellows who love Esmeralda. I can get them to create a disturbance outside Notre Dame, and while the soldiers are distracted with them, we can get inside and rescue her."

"Splendid! Splendid! Esmeralda will soon be in our hands . . . rescued, of course. Go now, Master Pierre, and get your friends ready for the attack tonight."

184

"I Have an Idea!"

THE HUNCHBACK OF NOTRE DAME

Pierre hurried to the Court of Miracles and met with King Clopin in the tavern that evening. The king was delighted to organize the adventure, not only to rescue the gypsy girl, but to steal all the valuable gold and silver and jewels at Notre Dame as well.

Word went out all over Paris that the attack would begin at midnight, and within hours the Court of Miracles began filling up with thousands of men, women, and weapons.

When the Court was overflowing, Clopin stood up on his barrel throne and told the crowd, "We'll go in a single line and in silence. No one is to light a torch until we get there."

While Clopin was organizing his army, the hunchback was making his midnight rounds in the church, locking the thick, heavy doors with their huge iron bars. When that was done, he climbed to the top of the northern tower and stood for a long while looking out over Paris. He had been a little uneasy for several hours after noticing some suspicious men

Clopin on His Barrel Throne

prowling around the church, looking up at Esmeralda's room. "If anyone's planning some treachery against her, I must be on my guard constantly to protect her."

Even though he had only one eye, that eye was sharp. With the entire city now in darkness, that eye spotted a line of heads walking towards the cathedral. Within minutes, the square was filled with thousands of silent bodies. Although Quasimodo wasn't the smartest of creatures, his brain began to reason with amazing speed. "Shall I waken Esmeralda? Get her out of the church? But how? The streets are filled. The church is at the edge of the river and there are no boats here at this time of night. No, I must fight here to the death, but not disturb my beautiful Esmeralda."

At a signal which Quasimodo couldn't hear, thousands of torches were lit, revealing a frightful army of ragged men and women armed with sickles, axes, pruning-hooks, spears and pitchforks.

A Frightful Army

THE HUNCHBACK OF NOTRE DAME

King Clopin held a whip in one hand and a torch in the other as he climbed up on a post and turned towards Notre Dame. "Hear me, Bishop of Paris!" he called out. "One of our sisters was falsely accused of witchcraft and has taken refuge in your church. You granted her sanctuary, and now you are letting her be arrested tomorrow. We order you to surrender her to us. If you don't, we'll come in and take her, along with everything of value in your church!"

Quasimodo had gone down to the lower platform between the two towers to get a better look at the attackers. While he saw Clopin talking and waving his arms, he couldn't know what the man was saying and he imagined the worst. "They're here to harm Esmeralda! I must save her even if it costs my life!"

When Clopin had no reply from inside Notre Dame, he ordered, "Forward, brothers!"

Thirty men moved out of the crowd and up

"Forward, Brothers!"

the steps to the central door of the church. They began attacking it with hammers, pincers, and crowbars, but the door was too strong. Just as more men approached with more tools, a huge beam fell from the sky, crushing dozens of men on the steps. Those still standing scattered in terror.

"It's the moon attacking us!" cried one superstitious man.

"It's the devil!" cried others.

"You're all a pack of fools!" shouted Clopin, but he couldn't explain where the beam came from either, for the light from their torches didn't reach up high enough. "It's the priests defending themselves," he cried, offering some explanation to his men. "Forward again!"

But when the men didn't move, he argued, "Are you afraid of the beam?"

An old gypsy called out, "It's not the beam, your majesty. The door is bolted with heavy iron bars. Our pincers are useless. We need a battering-ram to break it open."

A Beam Fell From the Sky

THE HUNCHBACK OF NOTRE DAME

"And you've got one!" exclaimed Clopin as he pointed to the huge beam. "God sent it!"

With new courage, a hundred men lifted the beam and crashed it furiously against the thick door. The crash shook the entire cathedral, but the door didn't give way.

Just then, a shower of boulders began to fall on the attackers. But as each man fell from blows to his head, another took his place at the battering-ram.

High above, brave Quasimodo was the lone defender of Esmeralda and Notre Dame. He had climbed to the high tower and his weapons were the building materials workmen had stored there as they repaired the church roof during the day. There were piles of rough stones, rolled-up sheets of lead, bundles of wood strips, and heaps of debris.

With superhuman strength, he pushed heavy beams through the windows, lifted and rolled boulders over the platform, and flung stones and iron tools by the handfuls onto the

Brave Quasimodo, the Lone Defender

men one hundred sixty feet below. With each successful hit, Quasimodo grunted loudly and laughed ferociously.

But the door was weakening and Quasimodo's supply of weapons was quickly dwindling. Then he had an idea. The water spouts on two of the gargoyles opened directly onto the front of the cathedral where the men were battering the door. Just behind the gargoyles was a huge pot in which the workmen melted the lead used to waterproof the roof. Quasimodo gathered piles of sticks and started a fire under the pot, adding the sheets of lead to the pot as it heated.

During the lull while the lead was melting, Quasimodo spotted a group of men starting to climb a tall ladder they had pushed against the wall below the lower gallery. He ran down the steps and when all the rungs were filled with attackers, the powerful hunchback gripped the top of the ladder in his huge hands. With superhuman strength, he pushed

Starting a Fire!

it back from the wall and sent it crashing down to the square below. A frightful uproar of screams and curses followed, then only moans and groans as a few bloody survivors crawled out in agony.

Quasimodo then returned to the tower to his huge pot. The lead was boiling. It was ready. But the door was also ready . . . ready to crash in. Gathering all the strength in his deformed body, Quasimodo pushed against the pot until it began to tip over, spilling its boiling lead towards the water spouts.

Without warning, the mouths of the two monstrous gargoyles began spitting out streams of burning lead onto the men directly below. Most of them were killed instantly; the rest shrieked and groaned in agony, as they fled wildly, their flesh burning!

But soon, more ladders and ropes appeared, and the army of men, enraged now by the attacks on their comrades, began scaling the walls of the cathedral on all sides.

Streams of Burning Lead

THE HUNCHBACK OF NOTRE DAME

"The church is about to fall to them!" cried Quasimodo as he ran back and forth. "I must save Esmeralda!"

Suddenly, the clatter of hundreds of horses filled the square. Clopin's army turned in terror and confusion as government soldiers attacked with spears and lances. The thieves, beggars, and gypsies were no match for the well-armed soldiers. They finally gave up the fight and fled in all directions.

Quasimodo, who had continued his fight all this time, fell to his knees, overjoyed that the attackers were gone, chased away by men who had come to rescue her. He was certain that he had saved Esmeralda once again from those wishing to harm her. His one thought now was to bring her the good news.

He hurried up to the tower and burst into her room. But to his horror, it was empty!

It Was Empty!

Two Men Were at the Door.

CHAPTER 15

My Mother! My Daughter!

When the attack on Notre Dame began, Esmeralda had been asleep. But the noise of the fighting and the bleating of her little goat soon woke her. She rushed out of her room and looked down into the square from the tower. Seeing the fierce attack, she once again feared for her life and feared that she'd never see Phoebus again.

She hurried back to her room and threw herself on her bed, frozen with fear. Soon, she heard footsteps. Two men were at the door, the first holding a lantern.

"Don't be afraid, Esmeralda. It is I, your husband, Pierre Gringoire."

"Who's that with you?" she asked, pointing to a figure all in black behind him.

"Don't worry. He's a friend of mine. . . . Ah, here's my dear, sweet goat." And he put down the lantern so he could hug Djali.

But when the man in black pulled him to his feet, Pierre snapped at him, "I know we're in a hurry, but you needn't shove me around. . . . Now, my dear girl, as I was saying, your life is in danger. So is Djali's. The men outside have orders to arrest you, and we've come to save you."

The man in black picked up the lantern and turned to the door. Pierre took Esmeralda by the hand and led her and the goat down the tower stairs behind his companion.

Once they were out in the dark, deserted courtyard, the man in black walked straight to the bank of the river, where a small boat was hidden behind a fence. He motioned for Pierre,

"It is I, Pierre Gringoire."

Esmeralda, and the goat to get in, then he climbed in with his back to them and pushed off from shore with a long boat hook.

As the girl sat huddled beside Pierre, who held the goat lovingly in his arms, the boat moved slowly to the right bank of the river.

With each hard pull of the oars, the man in black heaved a sigh. It was a strangely familiar sigh that somehow filled Esmeralda with a secret terror.

But the shouting voices from Notre Dame carried across the river, distracting her. "Death to the gypsy girl! Death to the witch!" Looking back, she saw torches burning brightly and soldiers swarming over the church from top to bottom.

A jolt signaled that the boat had reached shore. The stranger climbed out and tried to take Esmeralda's arm to help her, but the girl shook his hand off and got out by herself. Before she had a chance to turn around to get Djali, the boat had disappeared into the night,

The Man in Black

along with Pierre and her goat.

Esmeralda shuddered to find herself alone with the man in black. She tried to cry out, but no sound came from her throat. Suddenly she felt a strong, cold hand in hers, a hand that was dragging her along the street. She looked around for help, but the street was deserted. Breathless from trying to keep up with him as he ran uphill, she gasped, "Who are you? What do you want of me?"

The man in black didn't stop and didn't answer until they reached a large square with a scaffold and gallows in the center. Esmeralda finally recognized where they were and who the man was.

"We've come to the end, to the Place de Gréve!" said the cold, menacing voice of Dom Claude Frollo. "Your life is in my hands now, for only I can save you from this death." And he pointed to gallows atop the scaffold. "I can turn you over to the soldiers who are still searching for you or I can give you back your life."

"Your Life is in My Hands Now!"

He dragged the frightened girl closer to the scaffold and, pointing to the rope, he continued, "I love you. It's time now to make a choice. The hangman's noose or me?"

Esmeralda pulled away from him. Throwing herself at the foot of the steps, she cried, "Hanging isn't as horrible a death as being with you would be!"

The archdeacon lowered his arm and spoke as if in a daze. "I love you, can't you see that? My suffering is unbearable. Can't you forgive me and not hate me so?" He hid his face in his hands and began to weep uncontrollably. "I don't want to see you die. I can save you if you'll just forgive me and try to learn to love me one day."

"Love a murderer? Never!"

The crazed archdeacon grabbed the girl and shrieked, "Yes, I *am* a murderer! And you'll either die or run away with a murderer!"

"You filthy, disgusting monster! I belong to Phoebus. It's Phoebus I love. It's Phoebus

"Love a Murderer? Never!"

who's handsome. It's you who are ugly!"

"Then you'll die!" he screamed. And he began dragging her across the square to the stone cell of the old recluse.

"Gudule!" he called. "Here's the gypsy girl. You can now have your revenge! Hold her while I go for the soldiers."

As soon as a strong, bony arm reached out through the bars of the window and gripped the girl's elbow, the archdeacon ran off toward the bridge leading to Notre Dame.

"They're going to hang you!" cried Gudule with a sinister laugh. "Then I'll have my revenge against you gypsies for stealing my baby . . . my little girl who would have been your age now, if they had let her live."

"Have mercy on me!" cried Esmeralda as she struggled to free herself from the woman's incredibly strong grip. "I've done nothing to you. Let me escape, please!"

"First give me back my child!"

"You're looking for your child, and I'm

"Let Me Escape, Please!"

looking for my parents," begged Esmeralda. "Have pity on me!"

"Do you know where my little girl is? All I have is her shoe." With her free arm, Gudule held out the little embroidered shoe to Esmeralda. "It's all the gypsies left behind when they stole her away."

In the gray light of dawn, Esmeralda stared, unbelieving, at the shoe. "Oh, my God!" she cried, trembling. With her free hand, she hurriedly opened the little green bag around her neck and pulled out a little shoe. It was the mate to the one the old woman had been worshipping for fifteen years!

Seeing the shoes side by side, Gudule began to tremble. "Oh, my daughter! My precious baby!" she cried.

Esmeralda wept with joy. "My mother! My mother! At last I've found you!"

With tears streaming down their faces, Esmeralda reached her hands inside the bars, and Gudule pressed them to her lips.

"My Precious Baby!"

THE HUNCHBACK OF NOTRE DAME

Then suddenly, the old woman gripped the bars and began to shake them furiously until they had loosened slightly. She picked up a large stone from the floor of her cell and threw it against them with such strength that the bars cracked. With her hands summoning up superhuman strength, she bent back the remaining bars, then reached out and pulled her daughter into the cell. "Come here, my child. I'll save you now."

Once Esmeralda was inside, the woman picked her up in her arms and carried her back and forth as though she were still a baby, kissing her, singing to her, laughing and weeping all at the same time.

"My daughter! My daughter! God has given her back to me! We'll go far away from here. We'll be so happy."

"Oh, my mother!" cried the girl when she was finally able to speak. "What joy to have found you! Before her death, the good gypsy woman who raised me told me to wear this

Laughing and Weeping

bag around my neck, that it would lead me to my mother one day. And she was right. It did!"

Just then, the sound of clanging weapons and galloping horses reached their ears.

"Save me, Mother!" cried Esmeralda. "I'm afraid. They're coming after me!"

"God in heaven, what have you done?"

"Nothing, but the priest and the court, they've sentenced me to death!"

"Death!" gasped Gudule, staggering back against the wall. "No, I can't lose you now after finding you again, so beautiful and so grown up. No, it's not possible. They can't take you away from me. Quick, hide in the corner. It's dark there. I'll tell them you escaped. I'll send them away. Just stay there quietly."

A loud voice outside the window called, "This is where the archdeacon said we'd find her, Captain Phoebus."

"I'm coming."

The effect of that voice on Esmeralda cannot be described. "He's my friend, my love. He'll

"Save Me, Mother!"

protect me," she whispered to herself. Then she jumped up and, before her mother could stop her, she ran to the window and cried out, "Phoebus, my love! Here I am!"

Her mother threw herself at the girl and pulled her back. But it was too late.

"Move aside, old woman! I want the other one, not you." It was the hangman, and he held a thick coil of rope in his hands.

"There's no other one here!" cried the old woman frantically. "I'm alone here."

"Go in and get the girl!" ordered the captain. "I heard her voice and saw her."

"But there's no door," said the hangman, embarrassed.

"Then break down the wall around the window and go in that way. Do it now!"

It didn't take long for the pick-axes and crowbars to start removing the large stones from under the window. Gudule was running around the cell, her eyes flaming. Then she suddenly picked up a stone and, laughing

"Break Down the Wall."

madly, hurled it at the soldiers. It landed harmlessly at the feet of Captain Phoebus's horse. Helpless to do anything more, the old recluse sat down beside her daughter and covered the girl with her own body.

Still in a daze, Esmeralda sat there, murmuring over and over, "Phoebus! Phoebus!"

Wild-eyed and foaming at the mouth, Gudule started crawling on all fours. "I'll never let you take my daughter! Never!"

"Remove the last stone!" came the order.

As six strong men with crowbars began to raise the heavy stone, the woman threw herself on it, scratching it with her fingernails. But the stone slipped away from her and rolled to the ground outside her cell.

She tried to block the entrance now with her frail body, but seeing three strong soldiers approach, she dropped to her knees and begged, "Gentlemen, this is my lost daughter. I've been separated from her for fifteen years and we've just found each other again after all

Blocking the Entrance with Her Frail Body

that time. I believed she was dead, but she wasn't. It's God's miracle. If you must take someone, take me. She's barely sixteen and has a lifetime ahead of her. Gentlemen, remember your mothers, remember how they loved you! Let me keep my child. I'm begging you on my knees!"

In spite of her words, her tears, her moans, her sighs, and her agonizing cries, Phoebus leaned over to the hangman and said in a low voice, "Get it over quickly!"

The hangman and three soldiers entered the cell. The mother threw herself across her daughter. When the girl realized the horror of what was happening, she stopped murmuring Phoebus's name and cried out, "Mother! Don't let them take me! Keep them away from me!"

As the hangman seized Esmeralda, she let out a weak cry and fainted. He picked her up in his arms, but found he was also dragging her mother along with her, for the woman refused to let go of the girl's waist.

The Hangman Seized Esmeralda

THE HUNCHBACK OF NOTRE DAME

When he reached the foot of the steps leading up to the scaffold, the hangman stopped and tied a rope around the girl's neck. She opened her eyes suddenly and saw the gallows on top of the scaffold.

"No! No! I don't want to die!" she cried.

The hangman finally managed to pull the exhausted recluse away from the girl, and he began to climb the steps with her limp body over one shoulder. But Gudule rushed at him like a wild animal and sank her teeth into his hand. He screamed in pain until several soldiers rushed up and pulled her away. They threw her to the ground so violently that she struck her head on the pavement and lay there, dead!

The hangman continued his climb up the cold stone steps where the gallows awaited Esmeralda. . . .

Like a Wild Animal

Pounding His Head Against the Wall

CHAPTER 16

"Everything I Loved!"

When the soldiers entered Notre Dame, they found the hunchback running all over the cathedral, uttering strange cries and tearing his hair out looking for Esmeralda. Thinking they were there to help the girl, he led them to every possible hiding place he knew. But they found nothing and finally left.

Quasimodo returned to Esmeralda's room. His grief had become so intense that he pounded his head against the stone wall, over and over, with such force, that he knocked himself unconscious.

THE HUNCHBACK OF NOTRE DAME

Later, when he came to his senses, he sat hugging her mattress for over an hour, wondering who might have taken her away. "It must have been my master," he finally decided. "He *did* try to seize her once before and he's the only one with a key to the staircase leading up to her room." Then he cried out in sorrow and despair, "If it were any other man, I'd tear him apart with my bare hands! But I love Dom Claude. He's been like a father to me. What am I to do?"

By now, daylight was beginning to stream in through the window, and Quasimodo saw the archdeacon walking along the upper gallery of the cathedral. The priest stopped at the end of the gallery and stretched his neck to look out over the rooftops across the river.

Quasimodo went out after him, confused by his feelings of anger and love. The archdeacon had climbed up on the balustrade and was kneeling on it as he stared silently across the city.

Walking Along the Upper Gallery

THE HUNCHBACK OF NOTRE DAME

The hunchback came up behind him and followed the priest's gaze until he, too, was looking at the Place de Gréve ... at the scaffold and its gallows.

He saw a man carrying a young girl over his shoulder as he climbed the steps up to the scaffold. The thick rope tied around her neck trailed behind her long black hair.

Quasimodo caught his breath, then gasped, "Oh, no! It's Esmeralda!"

Once on the platform, the man tossed the rope over the arm of the gallows, then gave it a tug. When he stepped back, the girl's body was swinging at the end of the rope.

Suddenly, a terrible laugh burst from the archdeacon's throat. Quasimodo didn't hear the laugh, but he saw it. Rage and horror over that laugh twisted the poor hunchback's face even worse than nature had done years earlier. An animal roar left his throat as he lunged furiously at Dom Claude and, with a mighty push, sent him off the balustrade.

A Mighty Push

THE HUNCHBACK OF NOTRE DAME

The archdeacon managed to grab onto the head of a gargoyle just below where he had been kneeling. He clung to the stone creature desperately, looking up at Quasimodo who could have saved him merely by reaching out his hand. But the hunchback wasn't even looking at the pleading man below him. His one sad eye was fixed on the Place de Gréve, on the gallows, on the gypsy girl. A long stream of tears began to flow uncontrollably from that one deformed eye.

Terror gripped the archdeacon as he felt his body writhe in agony and his hands begin to slip. The next instant, his hands slid down the stone face of the gargoyle and he hurtled down to the ground two hundred feet below.

Quasimodo continued to weep as he gazed from the gypsy girl dangling at the end of the rope to the priest lying in the square below. A chilling sob burst from his chest and he cried out, "Oh! Everything I loved!"

Clinging Desperately

An Open Graveyard

CHAPTER 17

Together in Death

When Esmeralda's body was cut down from the gallows, it was taken outside the city to Montfaucon, a huge, ancient building whose tall stone pillars were all that remained standing. The building had once been the most famous gallows in Paris, but had now become an open graveyard for disposing of all bodies hung in the city. It was on a pile of rotting bodies and skeletons that Esmeralda was thrown.

As for Quasimodo, he simply disappeared from Paris and from Notre Dame on the day that the archdeacon and Esmeralda died. He was never seen again and no one ever knew what became of him.

A year later, however, some men were sent to Montfaucon to bring back the body of a political prisoner who had been pardoned after his death and allowed a proper burial. The men found a strange sight among the hideous corpses in that open graveyard. Two skeletons lay together in death, one embracing the other. One was the skeleton of a woman, with a little green silk bag around her neck. The other, which was holding the woman tightly in his arms, was the skeleton of a man. He had a twisted spine, one leg shorter than the other, and a hump on his back. His neck wasn't broken, so he hadn't been hanged. He had apparently just come there and died.

When the men tried to pull his skeleton away from the one in his arms, it crumbled into dust. . . .

Together in Death